Ten for Ten
Top 10 Tips to Make Cash

Carla O

ACKNOWLEDGMENTS

I'd like to thank God for His faithfulness and generosity in the intellectual as well as the physical realm.

Credit must be given to some of the great thinkers and adventurers of my generation. Seth Godin and Tony Robbins have each had an influence on stretching the boundaries of what we think is possible. Thank you. Audacious mentors create courageous artists.

Ten For Ten

Top 10 Tips to Make Cash

I'll never forget that day. I had been

working for years in an admin position just

squeaking by . One of our clients was

making conversation commenting on the

current state of daycare costs and that it

was "serious coin".

Right then and there I decided that when it

came time for my turn, I wouldn't settle for

anything less than making "serious

coin" working precisely the hours and type

of work that I chose.

Developing extra streams of income

became a hobby for me. I

am sharing some of my best ten tips to

produce extra cash to supplement you and

your family's lifestyle. Raising four

children in the 90's as well as after Y2K

would take every ounce of my creativity to

juggle the demands of parenting and

prospering.

I've come to realize that many of you will

benefit from my years of trial and error. I

made many surprising discoveries;

figuring out not only how to save money,

but increase and vary my income streams in

unconventional ways.

Maybe you are stuck at home, because of a

physical or health challenge or simply

because you have chosen to stay home to

raise your children. You know that your

work ethic is still alive and strong, if only

you could figure out how to make money

outside of a traditional 9-5 job. This book

was written for you.

So how did I start? I needed to find ways

and means to earn extra money while my

young children were still at home.

So what can a person to do with little or no

start up costs? I developed 10 straight

forward ways to bring more

unconventional money into your family's

wallet, and to stem the flow of money going

out. This just might translate into you

and your family having more money at the

end of the day. Most of us need more money

to save, to invest and to

maintain an enjoyable standard of living

now and in the years to come.

Without further ado, permit me to start.

Tip #1

Buy something from one thrift store and sell

it to another. I couldn't believe it when this

actually worked. I had scored a

beautiful brass horse themed item at a rock

bottom price at a local thrift shop. I knew

instinctively that it could sell for much more

than I bought it. So I ducked into the door

of the nearest antique shop and resold it to

the store's owner whose wife happened to

be a "horse" themed knick knack

collector.

There is unlimited potential in this strategy!

Tip #2

Cutting grass, shoveling snow and raking

leaves are three homeowner duties that

most of us want to try to get out of

doing....so many folks are more than happy

to pay a neighbor to do any of those duties.

If you are one of those individuals

that enjoys shoveling snow or cutting the

grass or raking leaves, don't be shy to share

your talents with the neighbors.

They will appreciate your help and won't

resent sharing some quick cash with you for

your efforts. Most grass cutting

involves using the lawnmower that belongs

to the home owner, so you won't have to

concern yourself with any upfront costs.

Snow shoveling may involve the purchase of

a low cost wide snow shovel that is ideal for

snowy days. Raking leaves may require the

purchase of a low cost rake. Snow shovels

and rakes are sometimes available at thrift

shops, yard sales and even at shops like

"Habitat for Humanity". The

homeowners will be delighted with your help

and are usually happy to provide the leaf

bags.

Hand made flyers sown throughout the

neighborhood will help others know the

assistance that you are offering.

Tip#3

Start a blog. Every coin earned from a

thriving blog will add to your family's

bottom line. All of us have something that

we know how to do. Blogging about what

you know will be a new adventure in

creativity!

Maybe you can make the best chili in town,

or ice the best birthday cake. Maybe you

grow the best organic tomatoes in the

county.Maybe your photography skills are

worth blogging about. Blog about what you

know best and what you enjoy talking

about.

Write as if you are talking to the neighbor

over the fence. Readers all over the world

may be looking for your great ideas and

advice!

Blogger and Wordpress are two blogging

sites which will allow you to start blogging

for absolutely free. There may arise

optional elements, which might cost money,

but you can always politely decline from

using anything on your blog that

isn't free.

Site: https://wordpress.com

Site: https://www.blogger.com/home

Blogging may take time before bringing in a

legit income. Blog earnings really depend on

how much consistent effort is

poured into the blog and the type of ads

posted onto the blog. Online advertisers

such as "Adsense", will pay you based

upon the number of views that your blog

brings to their ads. It is fairly simple to learn

how to copy and paste ad codes onto a blog,

but it may be ideal for those who are already

a bit computer savvy or who have a good

tolerance for learning new computer skills.

Be sure to access assistance from someone

who has computer knowledge. You can

read tutorials you find on line or go on

"Youtube" to find video sessions explaining

how to format and post ads on a blog.

Tip #4

Start a teeny tiny home based business that

costs fifty bucks or less to start up.

Two small home based businesses that are

easy peazy to start up with little or no

money are: House cleaning and Dog

walking.

One trip to the dollar store with no more

than fifty dollars will grant you the basic

supplies needed to start a house cleaning

business. You set the hours, and you

provide the elbow grease to clean

homes/offices for folks who are too busy

to do so themselves. Ask around what the

going rates are for housecleaning and quote

a price that will match or beat it.

Word of mouth is your most powerful asset

when it comes to getting the word out that

you can be trusted with "man's best

friend". Your neighbors will gladly pay you to

watch or walk or check in on their pets if

they know and trust you.

Business cards are not usually even needed.

The pet owners provide all the food, treats

and leashes required.

You provide what you have..... namely time,

trustworthiness, and the ability to give their

beloved pet a safe stroll around the

block while they are away at work or out of

town.

Tip #5

Contests and on line competitions. There

are many contests that are

absolutely free to enter. Companies and

organizations sponsor contests in order

to gain publicity and to build up a spirit of

generosity and goodwill around their brand.

The first time you win a thousand dollars will

convince you that there just might be more

contests that you might win. Just be careful

about preventing identity theft which is

unfortunately a real threat. Don't enter

contests or on line competitions that can't

guarantee the safety of your personal

information. If you're not sure whether a

company or organization can be trusted

with your personal information such as your

tel# and address, then don't enter the

Contest. Consider using some of your

creative skills to enter contests, such as

poetry, creative writing, song writing,

photography or drawing contests. You never

know what you might win. Even if you win

items that you and your family

don't want or need, you can always sell your

prizes on line through Ebay or Craigslist or

at a local consignment shop.

Tip #6

Micro blogging sites: The most success I

have had with a micro blogging site that

actually brings in legit cash is "Bubblews". It

takes time to build readership, but the site

Is legit and pays via Paypal. Wait times can

be up to two months or more before

receiving payment, but it is run by good

folks.

Site: http://www.bubblews.com

Tip #7

Returning "Empties". Yes, I know.... sigh.

No one dreams of becoming a bottle

collector.

But the sheer number of folks and

charities that raise funds by collecting

empty alcoholic beverage containers should

convince you that there is legit

coin to be earned simply by returning

"Empties" to the nearest beer store for cash.

"Empties" are easily found near parks,

campsites, beaches and walking paths. In

our region the local hockey teams raise

funds for uniforms and team events by

going door to door collecting "Empties".

Even if you are personally not interested in

this endeavor, it is interesting to note that

several folks have funded their stock market

accounts simply through a consistent

bottling effort.

Tip #8

Music Reviews. It was a delight to discover

that small coin could be made by merely

listening to music online and writing

a casual but sincere review of the music into

a simple form online. The site I used most

recently was legit and paid via Paypal and is

called "Slice the Pie".

Site: https://www.slicethepie.com

Tip #9

Scour local yard sales and rummage sales

and learn that precious skill called "haggling"

which will help you score low

cost items that you can re-sell at a higher

price. When you master "haggling" you'll be

able to pay what YOU choose to

pay rather than whatever the seller has

posted. Then you can turn around and

re-sell those items online or through

consignment shops for a profitable price.

Just remember to account for the money

you spend on gas driving around to

yard sales, as it is one of the upfront costs of

your enterprise. Buy low and sell high. Save

the rewards.

Tip #10

Write an e-book with no upfront costs other

than the time and effort it takes to write it

and then easily "self publish" it. Even

if you don't own a computer, most libraries

offer state of the art computers to their

patrons at no cost. You can use

your library's computers to write a book

using one of their word processing

programs. If you are unsure how to

utilize it, just be bold and polite to ask the

librarians for assistance. Most librarians

love to demonstrate their computer

skills and pass on their knowledge to others.

The popularity of e-books has gained

powerful momentum.

Fortunately e-books are a thrifty mom's

best friend, as they can be written for

absolutely nothing. The only thing that may

take a bit more effort than the writing of the

book itself, is figuring out how the book

needs to be formatted before you upload it

to a free self publishing site. Some of

your friendly neighborhood librarians may

also help you with the formatting of your

book.

Same goes for creating an attractive book

cover. Some of the self publishing sites

available at the time of the writing of this

book are: Smashwords, Lulu, Createspace,

and Kindle Direct Publishing. Try one out

and see if you are comfortable and pleased

with the results. If not, try another

self publisher for your next book.

Remember that you needn't

write a 500 page novel. Self publishing

encompasses a wide range of styles,

lengths and genres of books. Write about

what you know. The finesse will come with

experience.

Experience is gained once you overcome

any fear of failure and do that which you

have not done before.

Site: https://www.smashwords.com

Site: https://www.lulu.com

Site: https://www.createspace.com/Index.jsp;jsessionid=6FFD157BF11880F34A3BC1BE9E534FC0.bf1be6e9b4b587f368f883dd5f37cd2d

Site:
https://kdp.amazon.com/signin?language=en_US

Summary

The above ten tips have unlimited potential,

hidden in plain sight. Decide to try just one

of the above ideas to generate more cash, I

hope you will give it your 100% effort

and focus. Although the ideas are relatively

simple, the accomplishment will only be

complete when you give it your

total focus and concentration.

The beauty of developing more than one

income stream, is that if one dries up, you

always have another. Therefore once

you have created one functional income

stream from the top 10 list above, consider

adding a second or third one to

your financial arsenal. Most of these ideas

can prosper in a down market or an up

market, in good or bad economic times.

Then you can consider turning some of your

newly found cash into dividend paying

stocks. But that's another story. Stay

tuned.

Celebration Time

So let's say that now you've come to master

at least one of the above "cash

making"ideas. Now what? Are you going to

hide the rewards under your mattress or

spend it all on bubblegum?

Let's discuss a few ways you can use the

rewards of your labor to increase even

more.

Consider the notion of investing. If you have

never considered investing, remember, that

it's a more accessible world now for

even the most modest and "newbie"

investors. You don't need

a university degree or even thousands of

dollars to get started in the

world of investing. Even one hundred

dollars in a discount brokerage can start you

on your path to making your money

work harder for you.

In life, there are times when you, physically,

mentally and spiritually have to work very

hard. The work is intense and

there is a high physical, mental, and

emotional cost to doing that kind of

work.

But there can also come a time where you

can learn how to make your money work

harder than you do.

I'm not telling you to quit your job and run

full speed into the stock market. I'm talking

about first, just dipping your toe into

the "idea" of beginning to invest even with

just one hundred dollars.

If you happen to think that it's not possible

to start with so little money, then you are

going to be pleasantly surprised.

D.I.Y. investors have proven over and over

again over the past decade that a successful

journey into the world of investing

can start with just a very wee bit of funding.

So, if you are still home bound and expect to

have time in which you can read and do

some good thinking and self led

learning, then please consider what I am

about to suggest.

First of all, I would recommend that you go

to your local library and see if there are any

user friendly entry level books on the

stock market that you can start with.

You may feel very intimated even by

mentioning the word "investing" when folks

around town see you clipping coupons

and shopping in thrift stores. But, at the end

of the day, "others" are not paying your

bills, and you owe it to yourself to

consider a wide range of financial

opportunities for you and for

your growing family.

I could suggest some big name authors in

the world of investing, but that might scare

you off, so I am just going to

say....start somewhere with books that are

written in a language style that you can

easily understand. I'm not talking about

being spoon fed with a book of cartoon

characters, but about choosing books that

are written in the level of language skills

that you know you can handle.

Then when your kids are having their naps,

or you have a spare 30 minutes...just grab

one of those books and keep a piece of

paper handy, to jot down some of the new

vocabulary you are going to learn. Write

down any new words having to do with

investing.....words like "stocks, bonds,

dividends, yield" as well as their

definition. Also write down any questions

that come up while you are reading.

Being willing to ask questions is going to

turbo boost your learning curve. Think

about who you know in your community

to whom you may direct your questions. Do

you have a relative who can coach you in

your quest to learn a little bit

about investing? Or perhaps you can do a

few searches on line to find some videos or

blogs that will help you understand the

material that you are reading about.

I'm not here to endorse one method of

investing over another.

Some folks just really are thrilled by real

estate investing. Others prefer stocks and

others, just bonds or ETF's. But my point

today, is that I want you to consider the

possibility that some pre-planned portion

of your income stream can be directed

towards an investment plan.

Yes, it may be surprising to hear that some

folks have gained great wealth simply by

investing all the money they gathered

by collecting "Empties" and funneling it into

the stock market.

It is possible.

When you have a large family and there are

many demands on your budget, such as

food, clothing, school supplies, church

events, rent or mortgage payments, utilities

and Christmas presents, it can be

intimidating to even consider the

expectation of yet another financial

"obligation". But I don't consider investing

an "obligation", but rather I consider it a

great opportunity that many moms and

housebound folks don't consider.

Well that's enough about investing for now.

Just be sure to consciously choose what

your extra income stream is going to

support. Don't let your kids use it up on

bubblegum or video games. Use it for

something that is going to bring blessing to

you and your family in the future.

Maybe use it to top up your college savings

for the children or plump up some of your

own retirement savings.

Incomes require guidance, or else they

disappear without any discipline.

You know what your goals are. By the

way...have you written down your goals?

Where is that list? Is it readily available for

you to review daily or weekly?

Your goals provide a framework upon

which to structure your life. Those who

don't plan their lives, wind up following the

plans of others.

Don't let your dreams and aspirations

expire just because you're busy and your

family or health concerns are demanding a

lot of your time.

Your dreams and goals belong to you, and

you should value them highly. When you

begin to consider the possibility that you

can make some or all of them come true,

your confidence will increase and you will

regain that hope and faith that your life is

going to be fun and adventurous.

So, now you've established at least one

functional income stream. You've also

chosen some ways in which you can

consider investing some or all of your

income stream. You've refreshed your

dreams and aspirations and written a list of

life goals that you're keeping in a handy

location for regular review.

I'd say that you are well on your way to

more adventure and accomplishment than

you could have imagined.

Believe in yourself and in your dreams. One

little step per day will give you a sense of

momentum and your dreams will eventually

become reality.....if you don't give up.

I'd like to thank you for spending this time

with me. It has been my pleasure to bring to

you these simple opportunities hiding in

plain sight.

Wishing you extravagant peace,

empowerment and prosperity!

Disclaimer:

The ideas and websites discussed in this

book are intended for conversational

purposes only. The author and publisher of

this book are not responsible for any results

or actions taken in response to the ideas

and websites mentioned in this

book. The author and publisher of this book

accept absolutely no liability for the ideas

represented and discussed in this book. All

financial and legal advice should be

obtained from licensed financial and legal

professionals.

NOTES

Set your goals into motion.....

_____

_____

_____

_____

_____

_____

_____

_____

_____

_____

_____

_____

_____

_____

_____

_____

_____

_____

www.ingramcontent.com/pod-product-compliance
Lightning Source LLC
Chambersburg PA
CBHW020708180526
45163CB00008B/2994